# "THIS IS REALLY A GREAT CITY (I DON'T CARE WHAT ANYBODY SAYS)"* 501 Famous Lines from Great (and Not-So-Great) Movies

Compiled and Edited by
John P. Fennell, with
additional lines by
Alvin H. Marill

*Woody Allen to Diane Keaton: MANHATTAN, 1979

A Citadel Press Book
Published by Carol Publishing Group

Editorial Offices
600 Madison Avenue
New York, NY 10022

Sales & Distribution Offices
120 Enterprise Avenue
Secaucus, NJ 07094

In Canada: Musson Book Company
A division of General Publishing Co., Limited
Don Mills, Ontario

Design by Steven Brower

Manufactured in the United States of America

10   9   8   7   6   5   4   3   2

Carol Publishing Group books are available at special discounts
for bulk purchases, for sales promotions, fund raising, or
educational purposes. Special editions can also be created to
specifications. For details contact: Special Sales Department,
Carol Publishing Group, 120 Enterprise Ave., Secaucus, NJ 07094

**Library of Congress Cataloging-in-Publication Data**

"This is really a great city  (I don't care what anybody says)":
501 famous lines from great (and not-so-great)
movies / compiled and edited by John P. Fennell.
    p.   cm.
    "A Citadel Press book."
    ISBN  0-8065-9980-4
    1. Motion pictures—Quotations, maxims, etc.   I. Fennell, John P.
PN1994.9Y68   1989
791.43'0207—dc20                                                                89-38194
                                                    CIP

This book is dedicated
to the late, great
**HARRY BALL**

# CONTENTS

# INTRODUCTION

"It's a beautiful city," Adolphe Menjou tells Ginger Rogers in *Stage Door* back in 1937, "Just like a fairyland—it's full of color, romance, illusion, glamour…" Menjou was speaking, of course, about New York. More than a half century has elapsed since Menjou spoke the line, but time has done nothing to alter his assessment. Today, New York is still a beautiful city. It still has color; it still has romance, illusion, glamour. And it has a lot more besides. For one thing, it has movies. Movies and more movies.

New York is where I became a movie junkie. The lines in this book reflect my addiction. They are not intended to be, as Hollywood might hype them, "The 501 Greatest Quotes of All Time!" Rather, they reflect this movie buff's personal favorites. By happy coincidence my selections include most, if not all, of the best-known movie lines of our time. The six decades of the "talkies"—from 1927 to 1990—are represented roughly proportionately. The Thirties and Forties have more quotes than the Seventies through 1990 because so many more movies were made back then. And while I recognize that quantity is certainly no guarantee of quality, even a cursory glance at the lines from those early decades argues eloquently for their inclusion. For better or worse, the final selections in this book are mine and mine alone.

While compiling the book, I found to my shock and chagrin that some of my most favorite movie lines were misquotes—or worse still, that they did not exist. For example, Cary Grant never said, "Judy, Judy, Judy," and Charles Boyer somehow forgot to say, "Come with me to the Casbah." Neither Humphrey Bogart nor Ingrid Bergman actually asked Dooley Wilson to, "Play it *again*, Sam." Nor did Mae West ever say, in so many words, "Come up and see me sometime," nor Gary Cooper drawl the exact phrase, "Smile when you say that." And, although I still will swear that I heard him say it in *some* movie, Jimmy Cagney never once snarled, "You dirty rat!" Yet these and other similarly jumbled lines continue to persist in my and many other moviegoers' imaginations and—well, who's to say they've done us any harm?

For my lifelong love affair with movies I have New York to thank. For over thirty-five years the city's numerous and varied movie houses were "just like a fairyland" to me. Ginger Rogers—again from *Stage Door*—expresses my sentiments best. "I love New York," she croons as she gazes down from Adolphe Menjou's penthouse, "...it looks so rouged, manicured, and ready to go out for the evening." To the movies, no doubt.

I wish to extend acknowledgements and thanks to Janet Bailey, David DePolo, Ken Luboff, Marion and H.L. Scarborough, Jennifer Golden, Heather and Tatiana Masters, and my two movie-loving sons, Morgan and Phineas. I would also like to acknowledge the contribution of Harry Haun's comprehensive and authoritative work, *The Movie Quote Book* (Lippincott & Crowell, 1980), which served as an invaluable source of research for this book. Leslie Halliwell's monumental *Film Guide* was also an immeasurable help as a research aid. The screenwriter William Goldman's *Adventures in the Screen Trade* was also informative as well as entertaining. Thanks are also owed to my brother Tom Fennell for his research assistance and for being there when it really counted. And to my wife Nancy I owe a special debt of gratitude, not only because of her constant support, encouragement, and editorial assistance, but most of all because she falls for a good line when she hears one, every time.

John P. Fennell
1991

1. "Wait a minute, wait a minute, you ain't heard nothin' yet! Wait a minute, I tell you. You ain't heard nothin' yet! Do you want to hear 'Toot, Toot, Tootsie'?"

> Al Jolson—first line in "talkies," in
> second reel of THE JAZZ SINGER, 1927

2. "A million lights they flicker there/A million hearts beat quicker there/There are no shades of gray/On the Great White Way."

> Charles King
> BROADWAY MELODY, 1929

3.. "If you want to call me that, smile."

> Gary Cooper to Walter Huston
> THE VIRGINIAN, 1929

# THE THIRTIES

4. "Gimme a visky with a chincher ale on the side—and don't be stingy, baby."

> Greta Garbo's first line on screen
> ANNA CHRISTIE, 1930

5. "They call me Lola."

Marlene Dietrich to Emil Jannings
THE BLUE ANGEL, 1930

6. "Would you be shocked if I put on something more comfortable?"
Jean Harlow to Ben Lyon
HELL'S ANGELS, 1930

7. "One morning I shot an elephant in my pajamas. How he got into my pajamas I'll never know."

Groucho Marx
ANIMAL CRACKERS, 1930

8. "Mother of Mercy, is this the end of Rico?"

Edward G. Robinson's dying words
LITTLE CAESAR, 1930

9. "Another fine mess you've got us in, Stanley."

Stan Laurel and Oliver Hardy's frequent refrain
Laurel & Hardy films, 1930s

10. "You'll have to forgive me, comrade."

Lew Ayres to the dead Raymond Griffith
ALL QUIET ON THE WESTERN FRONT, 1930

11. "It seemed like a good idea at the time."

Richard Barthelmess' oft-quoted line
THE LAST FLIGHT, 1931

12. "Ay yam — Drak-ku-lah...Ay bid you velcome!"

Bela Lugosi to Dwight Frye
DRACULA, 1931

13. Perhaps most famous visual line in movies.

James Cagney to Mae Clarke
THE PUBLIC ENEMY, 1931

14. "First the hunt, then the revels!"

Leslie Banks to his victim Joel McCrea
THE MOST DANGEROUS GAME, 1932


15. "I am Mata Hari, my own master."

Greta Garbo
MATA HARI, 1932

16. "(Me) Tarzan...(You) Jane."

Johnny Weissmuller to Maureen O'Sullivan
TARZAN THE APE MAN, 1932

17. "I can't help myself!"

Peter Lorre
M, 1932

18. "How do you live?"
"I steal..."

Paul Muni's haunting fadeout line
I AM A FUGITIVE FROM A CHAIN GANG, 1932

19. "We'll start with a few murders. Big men. Little men. Just to show we make no distinction."

Claude Rains's megalomania
THE INVISIBLE MAN, 1932

20. "I vant to be left alone."

Greta Garbo to John Barrymore
GRAND HOTEL, 1932

21. "It took more than one man to change my name to Shanghai Lily."

Marlene Dietrich to Clive Brook
SHANGHAI EXPRESS, 1932


22. "The white woman stays with me."

Warner Oland
SHANGHAI EXPRESS, 1932


23. "I'd love to kiss yuh, but I just washed mah ha-yer."

Bette Davis
CABIN IN THE COTTON, 1932

24. "Goodness, what beautiful diamonds!"
    "Goodness had nothing to do with it, dearie."

> Mae West to cloakroom girl
> NIGHT AFTER NIGHT, 1932

25. "It went for a little walk..."

> Bramwell Fletcher regarding the departed monster
> THE MUMMY, 1932

26. "Am I a king or a breeding bull?"

> Charles Laughton
> THE PRIVATE LIFE OF HENRY VIII, 1933

27. "Beulah, peel me a grape."

> Mae West to Gertrude Howard
> I'M NO ANGEL, 1933

28. "It's not the men in my life, but the life in my men."

Mae West
I'M NO ANGEL, 1933


29. "Go out there and be so swell you'll make me hate you."

Bebe Daniels to Ruby Keeler
42ND STREET, 1933


30. "I was reading a book the other day...the guy said machinery is going to take the place of every profession."
"Oh, my dear, that's something you'll never have to worry about."

Jean Harlow and Marie Dressler
DINNER AT EIGHT, 1933

31. "Is that a gun in your pocket or are you just glad to see me?"
Mae West to Charles Osgood
SHE DONE HIM WRONG, 1933

32. "Why don't you come up sometime 'n see me....I'm home every evening."

Mae West to Cary Grant
SHE DONE HIM WRONG, 1933

33. "Wa saba ani mako, O tar vey, Rama Kong."
(Translation: "The bride is here, O mighty one, great king.")

Witch Doctor presenting Fay Wray
KING KONG, 1933

34. "I hear it's a kind o' gorilla."
   "Ain't we got enough'a them in New York?"

   > Man and woman theatergoers on opening night of
   > Broadway's "Kong! Eighth Wonder of the World!"
   > KING KONG, 1933

35. "As long as they've got sidewalks, you've got a job."

   > Joan Blondell to Claire Dodd
   > FOOTLIGHT PARADE, 1933

36. "I suggest we give him ten years in Leavenworth or eleven years
   in Twelveworth."
   "I tell you what I'll do. I'll take five and ten in Woolworth."

   > Groucho Marx and Chico Marx
   > DUCK SOUP, 1933

37. "Box it."

Ned Sparks to Claudette Colbert
IMITATION OF LIFE, 1934


38. "Your wife is safe with Tonetti — he prefers spaghetti."

Erik Rhodes
THE GAY DIVORCEE, 1934

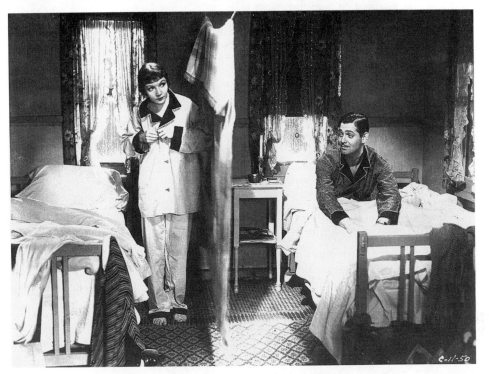

39. "A good night's rest'll do you a lot of good. Besides, you got nothing to worry about: the walls of Jericho will protect you from the big bad wolf."

Clark Gable to Claudette Colbert
**IT HAPPENED ONE NIGHT, 1934**

40. "We have ways of making men talk."

Douglass Dumbrille's oft-quoted line
LIVES OF A BENGAL LANCER, 1935

41. "You go. We belong dead."

Boris Karloff to Valerie Hobson
BRIDE OF FRANKENSTEIN, 1935

42. "Twas I informed on your son, Mrs. McPhillip. Forgive me."
Victor McLaglen to Una O'Connor
THE INFORMER, 1935

43. "If I'd have forgotten myself with that girl, I'd remember it."

Fred Astaire
TOP HAT, 1935

44. "The only fun I get is feeding the goldfish, and they only eat once a day!"

Bette Davis
BORDERTOWN, 1935

45. "I'll take my chances against the law. You'll take yours against the sea."

Clark Gable to Charles Laughton
MUTINY ON THE BOUNTY, 1935

46. "Hunger is an indulgence with these peasants as gout is with us."

Basil Rathbone's infamous hiss line
A TALE OF TWO CITIES, 1935

47. "Your dream prince, reporting for duty!"

Nelson Eddy to Jeanette MacDonald
ROSE MARIE, 1936

48. "Why <u>everybody</u> in Mandrake Falls is pixilated — except us."

Margaret Seddon to Gary Cooper
MR. DEEDS GOES TO TOWN, 1936


49. "Too many girls follow the line of least resistance."
    "Yeah, but a good line is hard to resist."

Helen Jerome Eddy and Mae West
KLONDIKE ANNIE, 1936


50. "I always look well when I'm near death."

Greta Garbo
CAMILLE, 1936


51. "Living, I'm worth nothing to her. But dead, I can buy her the tallest cathedrals, golden vineyards and dancing in the streets. One well-directed bullet will accomplish all that."

Leslie Howard to Humphrey Bogart
THE PETRIFIED FOREST, 1936

52. "Why did you two ever get married."
"Ah, I don't know. It was raining, and we were in Pittsburgh."

Barbara Stanwyck and Helen Broderick
THE BRIDE WALKS OUT, 1936

53. "I've got to have more steps. I need more steps. I've got to get higher...higher!"

William Powell's last delirious line
THE GREAT ZIEGFELD, 1936

54. "Not only is an innocent man crying out for justice; but more, much more—a great nation is in desperate danger of forfeiting her honor!"

Paul Muni's courtroom appeal
THE LIFE OF EMILE ZOLA, 1937

55. "I can tell you what an Indian will do to you, but not a woman."

Gary Cooper
THE PLAINSMAN, 1937

56. "I wouldn't go on living with you if you were dipped in platinum."

Irene Dunne to Cary Grant
THE AWFUL TRUTH, 1937

57. "Now that you've got the mine, I'll bet you'll be a swell gold digger."

Stan Laurel to Rosina Lawrence
WAY OUT WEST, 1937

58. "If I see your eyes, I might forget to be a king."

> Ronald Colman to Madeleine Carroll
> THE PRISONER OF ZENDA, 1937

59. "The calla lilies are in bloom again..."

> Katharine Hepburn's oft-quoted line
> STAGE DOOR, 1937

60. "You may as well go to perdition in ermine. You're sure to come back in rags."

> Katharine Hepburn to Ginger Rogers
> STAGE DOOR, 1937

61. "We have one simple rule here: Be kind!"

Sam Jaffe
LOST HORIZON, 1937


62. "He has a heart of gold — only harder."

Adolphe Menjou to Janet Gaynor
A STAR IS BORN, 1937


63. "Why are you wearing those clothes?"
"Because I just went gay all of a sudden."

May Robson discovering Cary Grant in a woman's robe
(coining a new usage?)
BRINGING UP BABY, 1938

64. "Cynthia...oh, she'll let you kiss her whenever you want. She doesn't want to swim. She doesn't want to play tennis, go for walks. All she wants to do is kiss you. I'm a nervous wreck!"

Mickey Rooney to Lewis Stone
LOVE FINDS ANDY HARDY, 1938

65. "I'm sorry, Pepe. He thought you were going to escape."
"And so I have, my friend."

Joseph Calleia and the dying Charles Boyer
ALGIERS, 1938

66. "You've all suffered from their cruelty—the ear loppings, the beatings, the blindings and hot irons, the burning of our farms and homes, the mistreatment of our women. It's time to put an end to this!"

Errol Flynn to peasants
THE ADVENTURES OF ROBIN HOOD, 1938

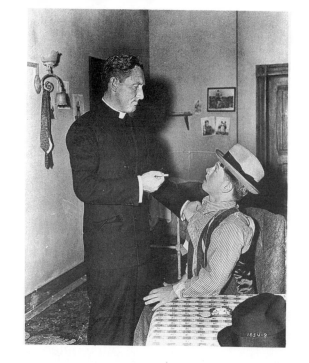

67. "Now, look, Whitey. In a pinch I can be tougher than you are, and I guess maybe this is the pinch. You're coming with me to Boys Town because that's the way your brother wants it and that's the way I want it."

Spencer Tracy to Mickey Rooney
BOYS TOWN, 1938

68. "I like my convictions undiluted, same as I do my bourbon."

George Brent
JEZEBEL, 1938


69. "Help me! I don't wanna die!"

James Cagney feigning fear
ANGELS WITH DIRTY FACES, 1938


70. "This neighborhood don't change much."

James Cagney talking about Hell's Kitchen in Manhattan
ANGELS WITH DIRTY FACES, 1938

71. "Take him to the tower and teach him the error of false pride."

> Eduardo Ciannelli to Victor McLaglen
> GUNGA DIN, 1939

72. "See them down there, coiling and wiggling, sticking their pretty tongues out..."

> Eduardo Ciannelli regarding snake pit
> GUNGA DIN, 1939

73. "Mad? ...Mad? ...Hannibal was mad, Caesar was mad, and Napoleon was surely the maddest of them all!"
Eduardo Ciannelli to Victor McLaglen and Douglas Fairbanks, Jr.
GUNGA DIN, 1939

74. "Toto, I have a feeling we're not in Kansas anymore."

Judy Garland in Oz
THE WIZARD OF OZ, 1939

75. "I'll get you, my pretty, and your little dog, too!"

Margaret Hamilton to Judy Garland
THE WIZARD OF OZ, 1939

76. "Pay no attention to the man behind the curtain...the...er...Great Oz has spoken!"

Frank Morgan to Judy Garland and friends
THE WIZARD OF OZ, 1939

77. "Toto, we're home...home...and this is my room, and you're all here...and I'm not going to leave here ever, ever again...because I love you all, and, oh, Aunt Em...there's <u>no</u> place like home!"

Judy Garland to all
THE WIZARD OF OZ, 1939

78. "I don't know nothin' 'bout birthin' babies, Miss Scarlett."

Butterfly McQueen to Vivien Leigh<br>GONE WITH THE WIND, 1939

79. "As God is my witness — as God is my witness — they're not going to lick me! I'm going to live through this, and, when it's all over, I'll never be hungry again — no, nor any of my folks! — if I have to lie, steal, cheat or kill! As God is my witness, I'll never be hungry again."

Vivien Leigh<br>GONE WITH THE WIND, 1939

80. "Frankly, my dear, I don't give a damn!"

Clark Gable to Vivien Leigh<br>GONE WITH THE WIND, 1939

81. "Tara! Home! I'll go home, and I'll think of some way to get him back. After all, tomorrow is another day."

Vivien Leigh
GONE WITH THE WIND, 1939

82. "If only I had been made of stone, like you."

Charles Laughton to gargoyle
THE HUNCHBACK OF NOTRE DAME, 1939

83. "That you, Martha?....I don't want to be disturbed."

Bette Davis' dying words to Virginia Brissac
DARK VICTORY, 1939

84. "That was restful...again."

Greta Garbo responding to Melvyn Douglas's kiss
NINOTCHKA, 1939

85. "Don't these big empty houses scare you?"
    "Not me, I was in vaudeville."

Nydia Westman and Bob Hope
THE CAT AND THE CANARY, 1939


86. "Somewhere, sometime, there may be the right bullet or the wrong
    bottle waiting for Josiah Boone. Why worry when or where?"

Thomas Mitchell
STAGECOACH, 1939

87. "I wouldn't give you two cents for all your fancy rules if, behind them, they didn't have a little bit of plain, ordinary, everyday kindness and a — a little looking out for the other fella, too."

Jimmy Stewart to Congress
MR. SMITH GOES TO WASHINGTON, 1939

88. "Oh, Watson, the needle."

Basil Rathbone to Nigel Bruce
THE HOUND OF THE BASKERVILLES, 1939

89. "Are you eating a tomato, or is that your nose?"

Charlie McCarthy (Edgar Bergen's voice) to W.C. Fields
YOU CAN'T CHEAT AN HONEST MAN, 1939

90. "She's got those eyes that run up and down men like a searchlight."
Dennie Moore about Joan Crawford
THE WOMEN, 1939


91. "Pity he had no children."
"Oh, but I have. Thousands of them. And all boys!"
Robert Donat rallying from his deathbed
GOODBYE, MR. CHIPS, 1939

92. "Take me to the window. Let me look at the moors with you once more, my darling. Once more."

Merle Oberon's dying words to Laurence Olivier
WUTHERING HEIGHTS, 1939

93. "Thank you, Mickey, and congratulations to you too."

Leopold Stokowski to Mickey Mouse
FANTASIA, 1940

94. "What symmetrical digits!"

W.C. Fields kissing Mae West's hand
MY LITTLE CHICKADEE, 1940

95. "There are but three things that men respect: the lash that descends, the yoke that breaks, and the sword that slays. By the power and terror of these you may rule the world."

Conrad Veidt infamous hiss line
THE THIEF OF BAGDAD, 1940

96. "Which would you prefer — New York or Manderley."

Laurence Olivier to Joan Fontaine
REBECCA, 1940

97. "I'm asking you to marry me, you little fool."

Laurence Olivier to Joan Fontaine
REBECCA, 1940

98. "Ze roo-bies, Bella...give me ze roo-bies"
Anton Walbrook to Diana Wynyard
ANGEL STREET (U.K. title GASLIGHT), 1940

99. "I jes trying to get on without shovin' anybody, that's all."
Henry Fonda
THE GRAPES OF WRATH, 1940

100. "Look up! Hannah! Look up!"

Charlie Chaplin
THE GREAT DICTATOR, 1940

101. "You're slipping, Red. I used to be frightened of that look—the withering glance of the goddess."

Cary Grant to Katharine Hepburn
THE PHILADELPHIA STORY, 1940

102. "I'm not happy...I'm not happy at all."

Walter Abel's frequent refrain
ARISE MY LOVE, 1940

103. "Some day, when things are tough, maybe you can ask the boys to go in there and win just one for the Gipper."

Ronald Reagan to Pat O'Brien
KNUTE ROCKNE—ALL AMERICAN, 1940

104. "By gad, sir, you are a character!!"

Sydney Greenstreet to Humphrey Bogart
THE MALTESE FALCON, 1941

105. "You will please clasp your hands together at the back of your neck."

Peter Lorre to Humphrey Bogart
THE MALTESE FALCON, 1941

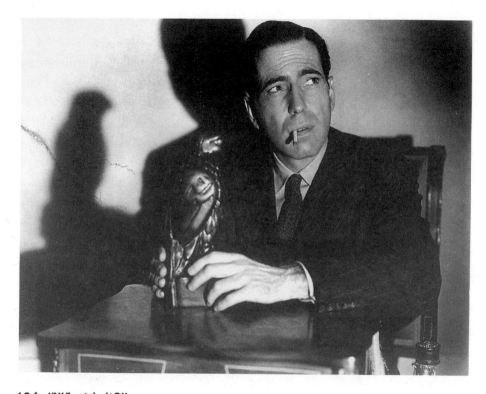

106. "What is it?"
   "The stuff that dreams are made of ..."
                    Ward Bond and Humphrey Bogart fadeout line
                          THE MALTESE FALCON, 1941

107. "See anything you like?"

Barbara Stanwyck to Henry Fonda
THE LADY EVE, 1941


108. "Yes, I killed him. And I'm glad, I tell you. Glad, glad, glad!"

Bette Davis laying it on thick
THE LETTER, 1941


109. "A soul? A soul is nothing. Can you see it? Smell it? Touch it? No…!"

Walter Huston to James Craig
ALL THAT MONEY CAN BUY, 1941


110. "This is where we change cars, Alvin. The end of the line."

George Tobias's dying words to Gary Cooper
SERGEANT YORK, 1941

111. "I run a couple of newspapers. What do you do?"

Orson Welles to Dorothy Comingore<br>CITIZEN KANE, 1941

112. "I guess Rosebud is just a piece in a jigsaw puzzle...a missing piece."

William Alland's fadeout line<br>CITIZEN KANE, 1941

113. "Hello, Monkey Face!"

Cary Grant to Joan Fontaine<br>SUSPICION, 1941

114. "I guess you are sort of attractive in a corn-fed sort of way. You can find yourself a poor girl falling for you if—well, if you threw in a set of dishes."

Bette Davis to Richard Travis<br>THE MAN WHO CAME TO DINNER, 1941

115. "She drove me to drink. That's the one thing I'm indebted to
     her for."

W.C. Fields
**NEVER GIVE A SUCKER AN EVEN BREAK, 1941**

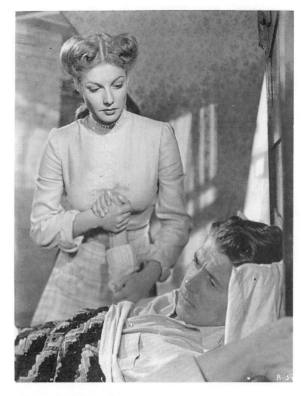

**116. "Where's the rest of me?"**
Ronald Reagan to Ann Sheridan regarding missing limbs
KINGS ROW, 1941

117. "Yes, I love him, I love those hick shirts he wears and the boiled cuffs and the way he always has his vest buttoned wrong. He looks like a giraffe, and I love him. I love him because he's the kind of guy who gets drunk on a glass of buttermilk, and I love the way he blushes right up over his ears. I love him because he doesn't know how to kiss—the jerk! I love him, Joe. That's what I'm trying to tell ya."

Barbara Stanwyck to Dana Andrews about Gary Cooper
BALL OF FIRE, 1941

118. "Mustard!"

Bette Davis to Jimmy Cagney
THE BRIDE CAME C.O.D., 1941

119. "Play it, Sam. Play 'As Time Goes By'!"

Ingrid Bergman to Dooley Wilson
CASABLANCA, 1942

120. "You played it for her, you can play it for me...If she can stand it, I can—play it."

Humphrey Bogart to Dooley Wilson
CASABLANCA, 1942

121. "Here's lookin' at you, kid."

Humphrey Bogard to Ingrid Bergman
CASABLANCA, 1942

122. "I stick my neck out for nobody."

Humphrey Bogart's credo
CASABLANCA, 1942

123. "People all say that I've had a bad break, but today — today
I consider myself the luckiest man on the face of the earth."

Gary Cooper to fans
THE PRIDE OF THE YANKEES, 1942

124. "Chivalry is not only dead, it's decomposing."

Rudy Vallee
THE PALM BEACH STORY, 1942


125. "Why don't you get out of that wet coat and into a dry martini?"

Robert Benchley to Ginger Rogers
THE MAJOR AND THE MINOR, 1942

126. "My mother thanks you. My father thanks you. My sister thanks you. And I thank you."

Jimmy Cagney to adoring audience
YANKEE DOODLE DANDY, 1942

127. "Your mother can't be with you anymore."

The Great Prince bringing the bad news to Bambi
BAMBI, 1942


128. "Now for Australia and a crack at those Japs!"

Errol Flynn's fadeout line
DESPERATE JOURNEY, 1942


129. "This is the people's war! It is our war! We are the fighters! Fight it, then! Fight it with all that is in us! And God defend the right!"

Henry Wilcoxon's film-ending sermon
MRS. MINIVER, 1942

130. "So they call me Concentration Camp Erhardt?"

Sig Rumann and Jack Benny's frequent refrain
TO BE OR NOT TO BE, 1942


131. "This is the screwiest picture I was ever in."

Talking camel to camera
ROAD TO MOROCCO, 1942


132. "You can't hurt me. I always wear a bullet-proof vest around the studio."

Elisha Cook's fadeout (punch) line
HELLZAPOPPIN, 1942


133. "I don't know how to kiss, or I would kiss you. Where do the noses go?"

Ingrid Bergman to Gary Cooper
FOR WHOM THE BELL TOLLS, 1943

136. "I've found peace in loving you. You shall have your house in Thornton Square."

Charles Boyer to Ingrid Bergman
GASLIGHT, 1944

137. "When I finish with my work, I wants my solitude and I wants my privitation."

Hattie McDaniel to Claudette Colbert
SINCE YOU WENT AWAY, 1944

134. "I can recommend the bait. I ought to know — I bit on it myself."

Tallulah Bankhead offering her diamonds for bait
LIFEBOAT, 1944

135. "Yes, I killed him. I killed for money and for a woman. I didn't get the money, and I didn't get the woman. Pretty, isn't it?"

Fred MacMurray confessing into dictaphone
DOUBLE INDEMNITY, 1944

138. "You know how to whistle, don't you, Steve? Just put your lips together and blow."

Lauren Bacall to Humphrey Bogart
TO HAVE AND HAVE NOT, 1944

139. "Anyone got a match?"

Lauren Bacall
TO HAVE AND HAVE NOT, 1944


140. "Why don't you get a divorce and settle down?"

Oscar Levant to Joan Crawford
HUMORESQUE, 1944

141. "Insanity runs in my family. It practically gallops."

Cary Grant to Priscilla Lane
ARSENIC AND OLD LACE, 1944

142. "Do you have a wee drop of the crature about?"

Bing Crosby to Barry Fitzgerald
GOING MY WAY, 1944

143. "It's lavish, but I call it home."

Clifton Webb to Dana Andrews
LAURA, 1944

144. "Did anyone ever tell you that you have a dishonest face — for a priest, I mean?"

Ingrid Bergman to Bing Crosby
THE BELLS OF ST. MARY'S, 1945

145. "Personally, Veda's convinced me that alligators have the right idea. They eat their young."

Eve Arden to Joan Crawford
MILDRED PIERCE, 1945

146. "Frederic, you must stop this Polonaise jangle!"

Merle Oberon to Cornel Wilde, the tubercular Frederic Chopin
A SONG TO REMEMBER, 1945

147. "What I'm trying to say is, I'm not a drinker — I'm a drunk."

Ray Milland to Jane Wyman
THE LOST WEEKEND, 1945

148. "Very stupid to kill the only servant in the house. Now we don't even know where to find the marmalade."

Judith Anderson
AND THEN THERE WERE NONE, 1945

149. "Ma'am, I sure like that name—Clementine."

Henry Fonda's last line to Linda Darnell
MY DARLING CLEMENTINE, 1946

150. "Tell me why it is that every man who seems attractive these days is either married or barred on a technicality."

Celeste Holm
GENTLEMAN'S AGREEMENT, 1946

151. "We are protected by the enormity of your stupidity."
Leopoldine Konstantin to Claude Rains as Ingrid Bergman listens
NOTORIOUS, 1946

152. "Alex, will you come in please? I wish to talk to you."

Ivan Triesault's ominous last words to Claude Rains
NOTORIOUS, 1946

153. "Pearl, you're curved in the flesh of temptation. Resistance is going to be a darn sight harder for you than for females protected by the shape of sows."

Walter Huston to Jennifer Jones
DUEL IN THE SUN, 1946

154. "You know, I've never been able to understand why, when there's so much space in the world, people should deliberately choose to live in the Middle West."

Clifton Webb
THE RAZOR'S EDGE, 1946

155. "I hate the dawn. The grass always looks as though it's been left out all night."

Clifton Webb
THE DARK CORNER, 1946

156. "Get me back. Get me back. I don't care what happens to me. Get me back to my wife and kids. Help me, Clarence. Please! Please! I wanna live again. I wanna live again! I wanna live again! Please, God, let me live again!"

Jimmy Stewart to Henry Travers
IT'S A WONDERFUL LIFE, 1946

157. "Speaking of horses...You've got a touch of class, but I don't know how — how far you can go."
"A lot depends on who's in the saddle."

Humphrey Bogart and Lauren Bacall
THE BIG SLEEP, 1946

158. "She tried to sit on my lap while I was standing up."

Humphrey Bogart
THE BIG SLEEP, 1946

159. "It is easy to understand why the most beautiful poems about England in the spring were written by poets living in Italy at the time."

George Sanders to Gene Tierney
THE GHOST AND MRS. MUIR, 1947

160. "I'm a ba-a-a-a-ad boy!"

Lou Costello's frequent refrain
ABBOTT & COSTELLO MOVIES, 1940s onward

161. "Susan's growing pains are rapidly becoming a major disease."

Myrna Loy to Rudy Vallee
THE BACHELOR AND THE BOBBY-SOXER, 1947

162. "You know what I do with squealers? I let 'em have it in the belly so they can roll around for a long time thinking it over."

Richard Widmark to Mildred Dunnock
KISS OF DEATH, 1947

163. "King Solomon had the right idea about work. 'Whatever thy hand findeth to do,' Solomon said, 'do thy doggonedest.'"

William Powell to James Lydon
LIFE WITH FATHER, 1947

164. "I just couldn't go to heaven without Clare. Why, I get lonesome for him even when I go to Ohio."

Irene Dunne about William Powell
LIFE WITH FATHER, 1947

165. "Now, wait a minute, Susie. Just because every child can't get its wish, that doesn't mean there isn't a Santa Claus."

Edmund Gwenn to Natalie Wood
MIRACLE ON 34TH STREET, 1947

166. "Botchess? We ain' got no botchess! We don't need no botchess!!
I don't half to show dju any stinkin' botchess!!!"

Alfonso Bedoya blowing his cover
THE TREASURE OF THE SIERRA MADRE, 1948


167. "Nobody ever put anything over on Fred C. Dobbs."

Humphrey Bogart
THE TREASURE OF THE SIERRA MADRE, 1948


168. "You're the most beautiful plank in your husband's platform."
"That's a heck of a thing to call a woman!

Adolphe Menjou and Katharine Hepburn
STATE OF THE UNION, 1948

169. "You shoulda let 'em kill me 'cause I'm gonna kill you. I'll catch up with you! I don't know when, but I'll catch up with you. And every time you turn around, expect to see me, because one time you'll turn around and I'll be there. I'll kill you, Matt."

John Wayne to Montgomery Clift
RED RIVER, 1948

170. "One Rocco more or less isn't worth dying for."

Humphrey Bogart regarding Edward G. Robinson
KEY LARGO, 1948


171. "You don't understand...every night when the moon is full, I turn into a wolf."
"You and fifty million other guys!"

Lon Chaney and Lou Costello
ABBOTT AND COSTELLO MEET FRANKENSTEIN, 1948


172. "Look, I can understand the temptation of a young man over here—but a grandfather! Really, Colonel Plummer, you should have your brakes relined."

Jean Arthur to Millard Mitchell
A FOREIGN AFFAIR, 1948

173. "I heard a scream, and I didn't know if it was me who screamed or not—if it was I or not."

Olivia de Havilland
THE SNAKE PIT, 1948

174. "I refuse to endanger the health of my children in a house with less than three bathrooms."

Myrna Loy to Melvyn Douglas
MR. BLANDINGS BUILDS HIS DREAM HOUSE, 1948

175. "What a dump!"

Bette Davis to Joseph Cotten
BEYOND THE FOREST, 1949

176. "In Italy for thirty years under the Borgias, they had warfare, terror, murder, bloodshed. They produced Michelangelo, Leonardo da Vinci, and the Renaissance. In Switzerland they had brotherly love, five hundred years of democracy and peace, and what did they produce — the cuckoo clock!"

Orson Welles to Joseph Cotten
THE THIRD MAN, 1949

177. "What can I do, old man? I'm dead, aren't I?"

Orson Welles to Joseph Cotten
THE THIRD MAN, 1949

178. "Never apologize and never explain — it's a sign of weakness."

John Wayne's credo
**SHE WORE A YELLOW RIBBON, 1949**

179. "Made it, Ma! ...Top of the world!"

James Cagney's dying words
**WHITE HEAT, 1949**

180. "New York, New York — it's a helluva town!"

> Gene Kelly, Frank Sinatra and Jules Munshin
> on beginning shore leave
> ON THE TOWN, 1949

181. "I suppose you know you have a wonderful body. I'd like to do it in clay."

> Lola Albright to Kirk Douglas
> CHAMPION, 1949

# THE FIFTIES

182. "When it bleeds — the Red Sea!"

Jose Ferrer regarding his nose
CYRANO DE BERGERAC, 1950

183. "Fasten your seat belts, we're in for a bumpy night."

Bette Davis to company
ALL ABOUT EVE, 1950

184. "Miss Caswell is an actress, a graduate of the Copacabana School of Dramatic Arts."

George Sanders to Bette Davis regarding Marilyn Monroe
ALL ABOUT EVE, 1950

185. "You're just not couth!"

Judy Holliday to Broderick Crawford
BORN YESTERDAY, 1950

186. "Crime is a left-handed form of human endeavor."

Sam Jaffe
THE ASPHALT JUNGLE, 1950

187. "I've wrestled with reality for 35 years, and I'm happy, Doctor. I finally won out over it."

Jimmy Stewart to psychiatrist
HARVEY, 1950

188. "I won't need that. He's a <u>young</u> lion."

Victor Mature to Hedy Lamarr
SAMSON AND DELILAH, 1950

189. "This floor used to be wood, but I had it changed. Valentino said, there's nothing like tile for the tango."

Gloria Swanson to William Holden
SUNSET BOULEVARD, 1950

190. "All right, Mr. DeMille, I'm ready for my closeup."

Gloria Swanson's fadeout line
SUNSET BOULEVARD, 1950

191. "That's quite a dress you almost have on."

Gene Kelly to Nina Foch
AN AMERICAN IN PARIS, 1951

192. "Some people are better off dead — like your wife and my father, for instance."

Robert Walker to Farley Granger
STRANGERS ON A TRAIN, 1951

193. "Nature, Mr. Allnut, is what we are put into this world to rise above."

Katharine Hepburn to Humphrey Bogart
THE AFRICAN QUEEN, 1951

194. "Pinch me, Rosie. Here we are, going down the river like Antony and Cleopatra on that barge!"

Humphrey Bogart to Katharine Hepburn
THE AFRICAN QUEEN, 1951

195. "You know what's wrong with New Mexico, Mr. Wedell? Too much outdoors. Give me those spindly trees in front of Rockefeller Center any day. That's enough outdoors for me."

Kirk Douglas
ACE IN THE HOLE, 1951


196. "I've met some hard boiled eggs, but you — you're twenty minutes!"

Jan Sterling to Kirk Douglas
ACE IN THE HOLE, 1951

197. "Hey, Stella!!...Hey, Stella!!!"

Marlon Brando yelling for Kim Hunter
A STREETCAR NAMED DESIRE, 1951

198. "Tell Mama. Tell Mama all."

Elizabeth Taylor placating Montgomery Clift
A PLACE IN THE SUN, 1951


199. "Among the gods, your humor is unique."

Leo Genn's understatement to Peter Ustinov
QUO VADIS?, 1951

200. "There's something about working the streets I like. It's the tramp in me, I suppose."

Charlie Chaplin to Claire Bloom
LIMELIGHT, 1952

201. "I believe that a man is fire and a woman fuel. And she who is born beautiful is born married."

Marlon Brando wooing Jean Peters
VIVA ZAPATA!, 1952

202. "It's no good. I've got to go back. They're making me run. I've never run from anyone before."

Gary Cooper to Grace Kelly
HIGH NOON, 1952

203. "I don't think Little Sheba's ever coming back, Doc. I ain't going to call her anymore."

Shirley Booth to Burt Lancaster
COME BACK LITTLE SHEBA, 1952

204. "A man's gotta dream; it comes with the territory."

Fredric March
DEATH OF A SALESMAN, 1952

205. "If we bring a little joy into your humdrum lives, it makes us feel our work ain't been in vain for nothin'."

Jean Hagen showing why she was best as a silent screen star
SINGIN' IN THE RAIN, 1952

206. "Only my friends call me 'wop.'"

Frank Sinatra to Ernest Borgnine
FROM HERE TO ETERNITY, 1953

207. "There is a pain beyond pain, an agony so intense, it shocks the mind into instant beauty."

Vincent Price to Phyllis Kirk
HOUSE OF WAX, 1953

208. "Prove it..."

Jack Palance's sinister refrain
SHANE, 1953

209. "Shane, come back...come back Shane!"

Brandon deWilde's fadeout line
SHANE, 1953


210. "Does this boat go to Europe, France?"

Marilyn Monroe
GENTLEMEN PREFER BLONDES, 1953


211. "A kiss on the hand might feel very good, but a diamond tiara is forever."

Marilyn Monroe
GENTLEMEN PREFER BLONDES, 1953


212. "Don't you think it's better for a girl to be preoccupied with sex than occupied?"

Maggie McNamara to David Niven
THE MOON IS BLUE, 1953

213. "Let me tell you what stooling is. Stooling is when you rat on your friends, the guys you're with."

Rod Steiger to Marlon Brando
ON THE WATERFRONT, 1954

214. "I could'a been a contender. I could'a had class and been somebody. Real class. Instead of a bum, let's face it, which is what I am. It was you, Charlie."

Marlon Brando to Rod Steiger
ON THE WATERFRONT, 1954

215. "Tell me lies."
"I have waited for you, Johnny."

Sterling Hayden and Joan Crawford<br>JOHNNY GUITAR, 1954

216. "Ah, but the strawberries! That's — that's where I had them. They laughed and made jokes, but I proved beyond a shadow of a doubt, and with geometric logic, that a duplicate key to the wardroom icebox did exist."

Humphrey Bogart telling more than he intends to Jose Ferrer<br>THE CAINE MUTINY, 1954

217. "Every street's a boulevard in old New York."

Dean Martin to Janet Leigh<br>LIVING IT UP, 1954

218. "Just this once, Kirk, why don't you empty your own ashtrays?"

Edmond O'Brien to Warren Stevens
THE BAREFOOT CONTESSA, 1954


219. "Harry, we must beware of those men. They're desperate characters...Not one of them looked at my legs."

Jennifer Jones to Edward Underdown
BEAT THE DEVIL, 1954


220. "Yonda is duh castle of my fodda."

Tony Curtis in unmistakable Brooklynese
THE BLACK SHIELD OF FALWORTH, 1954

221. "Take back your mink from whence it came!"

Vivian Blaine to Frank Sinatra
GUYS AND DOLLS, 1955

222. "What do you feel like doing tonight?"
"I don't know, Ange. What do you feel like doing?"

Joe Mantell and Ernest Borgnine's frequent refrain
MARTY, 1955

223. "Whenever someone else is crying, I've gotta cry too. I'm sympathetic. I've got too much of a heart."

Burt Lancaster to Anna Magnani
THE ROSE TATTOO, 1955

224. "'Man has a choice, and it's—the, the choice is what makes him a man,' see? You see, I do remember."

James Dean to Raymond Massey
EAST OF EDEN, 1955

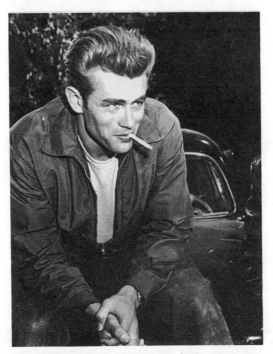

225. "Then the first thing that happens is I see you, and I thought this is going to be one terrific day so you better live it up, boy, 'cause tomorrow you'll be nothing."

James Dean's prophetic utterance to Natalie Wood
REBEL WITHOUT A CAUSE, 1955

226. "What seems to be the trouble, Captain?"

Mildred Natwick to Edmund Gwenn dragging a corpse
THE TROUBLE WITH HARRY, 1955

227. "Would you like a leg or a breast?"

Grace Kelly to Cary Grant
TO CATCH A THIEF, 1955

228. "We have not missed, you and I—we have not missed that
many-splendored thing."

William Holden to Jennifer Jones
LOVE IS A MANY-SPLENDORED THING, 1955

229. "Captain, it is I—Ensign Pulver—and I just threw your stinking palm tree overboard. Now, what's all this crud about no movie tonight?"

Jack Lemmon's fadeout line to Jimmy Cagney
MR. ROBERTS, 1955


230. "I wouldn't take you if you were covered in diamonds—upside down!"

Joan Crawford to Jeff Chandler
THE FEMALE ON THE BEACH, 1955


231. "I get so tired of just being told I'm pretty."

Kim Novak to William Holden
PICNIC, 1955

232. "I wanted to marry her when I saw the moonlight shining on the barrel of her father's shotgun."

Eddie Albert
OKLAHOMA!, 1955

233. "Et cetera, et cetera, et cetera."

Yul Brynner's frequent refrain
THE KING AND I, 1955

234. "Moses, you stubborn, splendid, adorable fool!"

Anne Baxter to Charlton Heston
THE TEN COMMANDMENTS, 1956

235. "Years from now, when you talk about this — and you will — be kind."

Deborah Kerr to John Kerr
TEA AND SYMPATHY, 1956

236. "Come on, darling. Why don't you kick off your spurs?"

Elizabeth Taylor to Rock Hudson
GIANT, 1956

237. "Oh, I see...the pellet with the poison's in the flagon with the dragon, the vessel with the pestle has the brew that is true."

Danny Kaye to Robert Middleton, trying to get it straight
THE COURT JESTER, 1956
(Same routine was used by Eddie Cantor in "Roman Scandals")

238. "If thee talked as much to the Almighty as thee does to that horse, thee might stand more squarely in the light."

Dorothy McGuire to Gary Cooper
FRIENDLY PERSUASION, 1956


239. "I don't know who I am anymore. I don't know what I remember and what I've been told I remember. What is real? Am I?"

Ingrid Bergman to Yul Brynner
ANASTASIA, 1956


240. "He rises!"

Gregory Peck regarding the white whale
MOBY DICK, 1956


241. "For me, there is no peace while you live, Mongol!"
"Say....yer beautiful in yer wrath!"

Susan Hayward and John Wayne
THE CONQUEROR, 1956

242. "The Tartar woman is for me, and my blood says, take her!"

John Wayne regarding Susan Hayward
THE CONQUEROR, 1956


243. "Wanna kiss me, Ducky?"

Marlene Dietrich to Charles Laughton
WITNESS FOR THE PROSECUTION, 1957


244. "Do you think it will ever take the place of night baseball?"

Deborah Kerr to Cary Grant
AN AFFAIR TO REMEMBER, 1957

245. "You give me powders, pills, baths, injections, and enemas—when all I need is love."

William Holden to Ann Sears
THE BRIDGE ON THE RIVER KWAI, 1957

246. "I'm adamant, I will not have an officer from my battalion working as a coolie!"

Alec Guinness to Sessue Hayakawa
THE BRIDGE ON THE RIVER KWAI, 1957

247. "We were just playing a game called Photography. You turn off the lights and see what develops."

Barry Coe
PEYTON PLACE, 1957

248. "I know you have a civil tongue in your head—I sewed it there myself!"

Whit Bissell to his creation
I WAS A TEENAGE FRANKENSTEIN, 1957

249. "Armies have marched over me."

Rita Hayworth
FIRE DOWN BELOW, 1957

250. "I'm not living with you. We occupy the same cage, that's all."

Elizabeth Taylor to Paul Newman
CAT ON A HOT TIN ROOF, 1958

251. "Life's never quite interesting enough, somehow. You people who come to the movies know that."

Shirley Booth to camera
THE MATCHMAKER, 1958

252. "A sculptor-friend of Auntie Mame's used this room for about six months. A divine man. Such talented fingers, but oh, what he did to my bust."

Rosalind Russell to Jan Handzlik
AUNTIE MAME, 1958

253. "It doesn't matter who gives them as long as you never wear anything second-rate. Wait for the first-class jewels, Gigi. Hold on to your ideals."

Isabel Jeans to Leslie Caron
GIGI, 1958

254. "Well, mustn't miss the old train, what, what? I must—I must stop saying 'What.' Cheeriebye. I must stop doing that too, I suppose."

David Niven to Wendy Hiller
SEPARATE TABLES, 1958

255. "New York you got air you can sink your teeth into. It has character. Jan, you can't live in Texas."

Tony Randall to Doris Day
PILLOW TALK, 1959

256. "Your eyes are full of hate, Forty-One. That's good. Hate keeps a man alive."

Jack Hawkins to Charlton Heston
BEN-HUR, 1959

257. "In spite of everything, I still believe that people are good at heart."

Millie Perkins's last lines
THE DIARY OF ANNE FRANK, 1959

258. "Killers kill, squealers squeal."

Jean-Paul Belmondo to Jean Seberg
BREATHLESS, 1959

259. "You gentlemen aren't really trying to murder my son, are you?"

Jessie Royce Landis to hit-men occupying same elevator
NORTH BY NORTHWEST, 1959

260. "Is your invitation to spread a little fertilizer still open?"

Gregory Peck to Ava Gardner
ON THE BEACH, 1959

261. "You don't understand, Osgood...I'm a man!"
"Well, nobody's perfect."

Jack Lemmon and Joe E. Brown's fadeout lines
SOME LIKE IT HOT, 1959

# THE SIXTIES

262. "Now, I may sound like a Bible-beater yellin' up a revival at a river-crossing camp-meeting, but that don't change the truth none."

John Wayne telling it like it is
THE ALAMO, 1960

263. "Why, we don't think a thing of a person's being Jewish, do we, Morris?"

Eve Arden protesting too much to Frank Overton
THE DARK AT THE TOP OF THE STAIRS, 1960

264. "Mother—what's the phrase?—isn't quite herself today."

Anthony Perkins to Janet Leigh
PSYCHO, 1960

265. "I love you, Spartacus."

Tony Curtis to Kirk Douglas
SPARTACUS, 1960


266. "Shut up and deal!"

Shirley MacLaine's fadeout line to Jack Lemmon
THE APARTMENT, 1960


267. "Mama, face it: I was the slut of all time."

Elizabeth Taylor to Mildred Dunnock
BUTTERFIELD 8, 1960

268. "And what is love? Love is the mornin' and the evenin' star..."
Burt Lancaster's frequent refrain
ELMER GANTRY, 1960

269. "Hello, Devil. Welcome to Hell."

Gene Kelly to Spencer Tracy
INHERIT THE WIND, 1960


270. "Eddie, you're a born loser."

George C. Scott to Paul Newman
THE HUSTLER, 1961

271. "Fat man, you shoot a great game of pool."

Paul Newman to Jackie Gleason
THE HUSTLER, 1961

272. "This, then, is what we stand for: truth, justice and the value of a single human being."

Spencer Tracy to courtroom
JUDGMENT AT NUREMBERG, 1961

273. "Cross my heart and kiss my elbow."

Audrey Hepburn's frequent refrain
BREAKFAST AT TIFFANYS, 1961

274. "Just head for that big star straight on. The highway's under it, and it'll take us right home."

Clark Gable's last line on screen to Marilyn Monroe
THE MISFITS, 1961

275. "Get up you scum suckin' pig."

Marlo Brando to desperado
ONE-EYED JACKS, 1961

276. "I'm not just talented. I'm geniused."

Rita Tushingham
A TASTE OF HONEY, 1961


277. "People who are very beautiful make their own laws."

Vivien Leigh to Warren Beatty
THE ROMAN SPRING OF MRS. STONE, 1961


278. "He's very progressive. He has all sorts of ideas about artificial insemination and all that sort of thing. He breeds all over the world."

Debbie Reynolds to Fred Astaire
THE PLEASURE OF HIS COMPANY, 1961


279. "Keep your pants on, Spartacus."

James Cagney to Horst Buchholz
ONE, TWO, THREE, 1961

280. "God bless Captain Vere!"

Terence Stamp to Peter Ustinov
BILLY BUDD, 1962


281. "Obedience without understanding is a blindness too — is that all I wished on her?"

Anne Bancroft regarding her pupil, Patty Duke
THE MIRACLE WORKER, 1962


282. "With Major Lawrence, mercy is a passion. With me, it is merely good manners."

Alec Guinness to Arthur Kennedy
LAWRENCE OF ARABIA, 1962

283. "He was a poet, a scholar and a mighty warrior...He was also the most shameless exhibitionist since Barnum and Bailey."

Arthur Kennedy eulogizing Peter O'Toole
LAWRENCE OF ARABIA, 1962

284. "Now look at me. I'm a bum. Look at me. Look at you. You're a bum. Look at you. And look at us. Look at us. C'mon, look at us. See? A couple of bums."

Jack Lemmon to Lee Remick
DAYS OF WINE AND ROSES, 1962

285. "I am not part of your luggage. Whatever I am, I am not part of your luggage."

> Paul Newman to Geraldine Page
> SWEET BIRD OF YOUTH, 1962

286. "Well, I suppose we'll have to feed the duchess. Even vultures have to eat."

> Shirley MacLaine
> THE CHILDREN'S HOUR, 1962

287. "That's my steak, Valance. Pick it up."

> Jimmy Stewart to Lee Marvin
> THE MAN WHO SHOT LIBERTY VALANCE, 1962

288. "Believe you me, if it didn't take men to make babies I wouldn't have anything to do with any of you!"

> Gena Rowlands exasperated with
> the recalcitrant cowpoke Kirk Douglas
> LONELY ARE THE BRAVE, 1962

289. "My name is Bond, James Bond."

Sean Connery's frequent refrain
James Bond movies, 1960s onward

290. "Boss, why did God give us hands? To grab. Well, grab!"

Anthony Quinn to Alan Bates
ZORBA THE GREEK, 1963


291. "Wake up, you country stewpot!...Rouse yourself from this pastoral torpor!"

Edith Evans to Hugh Griffith
TOM JONES, 1963

292. "Tom had always thought that any woman was better than none,
while Molly never felt that one man was quite as good as two."
Micheal MacLiammoir (narrator)
TOM JONES, 1963

**293. "There has never been such a silence..."**

Elizabeth Taylor regarding Richard Burton's death
CLEOPATRA, 1963

**294.** "Better wed than dead!"

Steve McQueen proposing to Natalie Wood
LOVE WITH THE PROPER STRANGER, 1963


**295.** "Sometimes I wonder whose side God's on."

John Wayne in an uncharacteristic moment of doubt
THE LONGEST DAY, 1963

296. "The only question I ever ask any woman is: 'What time is your
husband coming home?'"

Paul Newman to Patricia Neal
HUD, 1963

297. "There are worse things than chastity, Mr. Shannon."
   "Yes—lunacy and death."

Deborah Kerr and Richard Burton
THE NIGHT OF THE IGUANA, 1964

298. "Mr. President, I'm not saying we wouldn't get our hair mussed,
   but I do say not more than ten or twenty million killed tops,
   depending on the breaks."

George C. Scott to Peter Sellers
DR. STRANGELOVE, OR HOW I LEARNED TO STOP
WORRYING AND LOVE THE BOMB, 1964

**299.** "Mein Fuehrer! I can volk!"

Peter Sellers
DR. STRANGELOVE, OR HOW I LEARNED TO STOP
WORRYING AND LOVE THE BOMB, 1964

**300.** "Where the devil are my slippers, Liza?"

Rex Harrison's last line to Audrey Hepburn
MY FAIR LADY, 1964

301. "At our last meeting, I died. It alters the appearance."
Deborah Kerr to Felix Aylmer<br>**THE CHALK GARDEN, 1964**

302. "He has every characteristic of a dog except loyalty."
Henry Fonda to Lee Tracy regarding Cliff Robertson
THE BEST MAN, 1964

303. "Do you accept the protection of this ignoble Calaban on any terms that Calaban cares to make, or is your...eh, <u>delicacy</u> so exorbitant that you would sacrifice a woman and her child to it?"

Rod Steiger offering escape for Julie Christie
to a reluctant Omar Sharif
DOCTOR ZHIVAGO, 1965

304. "What happened?"
"Happened?...I didn't die. Everything that I loved was taken away from me and I did not die."

Rod Steiger trying to explain to Geraldine Fitzgerald
THE PAWNBROKER, 1965

305. "Your idea of fidelity is not having more than one man in bed at the same time."

Dirk Bogarde to Julie Christie
DARLING, 1965

306. "You dare to dicker with your pontiff?"

Rex Harrison to Charlton Heston
THE AGONY AND THE ECSTASY, 1965

307. "This is your neighbor speaking. I'm sure I speak for all of us when I say that something must be done about your garbage cans in the alley here. <u>It is definitely second-rate garbage</u>! Now, by next week, I want to see a better class of garbage. I want to see champagne bottles and caviar cans. I'm sure you're all behind me on this, so let's snap it up and get on the ball."

Jason Robards yelling out his window
A THOUSAND CLOWNS, 1965

308. "The world shall hear from me again..."

Christopher Lee
THE FACE OF FU MANCHU, 1965

309. "God always has another custard pie up His sleeve."

Lynn Redgrave
GEORGY GIRL, 1966

310. "My understanding of women goes only as far as the pleasures."

Michael Caine
ALFIE, 1966

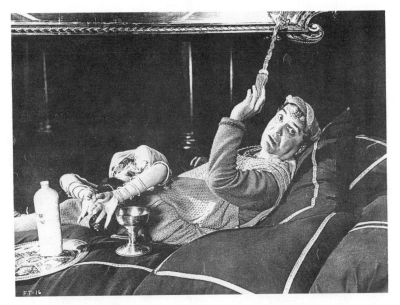

311. "Was 1 a good year?"

Zero Mostel's wine query
A FUNNY THING HAPPENED
ON THE WAY TO THE FORUM, 1966

312. "Too bad it didn't happen further down the street—in front of the May Company. From <u>them</u>, you can collect! Couldn't you have dragged yourself another twenty feet?"

Walter Matthau giving legal counsel to Howard McNear
THE FORTUNE COOKIE, 1966


313. "Oh, Richard, it profits a man nothing to give his soul for the whole world—but for Wales?"

Paul Scofield to John Hurt
A MAN FOR ALL SEASONS, 1966

314. "I swear, if you existed, I'd divorce you."

Elizabeth Taylor to Richard Burton
WHO'S AFRAID OF VIRGINIA WOOLF?, 1966

**315.** "Martha, will you show her where we keep the...er, euphemism?"

Richard Burton to Elizabeth Taylor regarding
Sandy Dennis's trip to the ...er, bathroom
WHO'S AFRAID OF VIRGINIA WOOLF?, 1966

**316.** "You know something, Virgil, you're the first person who's been around here to call....Nobody comes."

Rod Steiger to Sidney Poitier
IN THE HEAT OF THE NIGHT, 1967

317. "What we have here is a failure to communicate."

Strother Martin to Paul Newman
COOL HAND LUKE, 1967


318. "What's the going price on integrity this week?"

Orson Welles to Oliver Reed
I'LL NEVER FORGET WHAT'S 'IS NAME, 1967

319. "Mrs. Robinson, you're trying to seduce me, aren't you?"
Dustin Hoffman to Anne Bancroft
THE GRADUATE, 1967

320. "Plastics!"

> Walter Brooke advising Dustin Hoffman
> THE GRADUATE, 1967

321. "Well, Tillie, when the hell are we going to get some dinner?"

> Spencer Tracy's last line on film to Isabel Sanford
> GUESS WHO'S COMING TO DINNER, 1967

322. "I feel like we've died and gone to heaven — only we had to climb up."

> Mildred Natwick arriving breathless at
> Jane Fonda's fifth floor walk-up
> BAREFOOT IN THE PARK, 1967

323. "She cut off her nipples with garden shears. You call that normal?"

> Elizabeth Taylor to Brian Keith
> REFLECTIONS IN A GOLDEN EYE, 1967

324. "We rob banks."

Warren Beatty and Faye Dunaway
BONNIE AND CLYDE, 1967

325. "Stop—Dave. Will-you-stop? I'm afraid...I'm-afraid Dave. Dave. My-mind-is-going...I-can-feel-it. I-can-feel-it...There-is-no-question-about-it..."

Robot Hal's last line
2001: A SPACE ODYSSEY, 1968

326. "How could this happen? I was so careful. I picked the wrong play, the wrong director, the wrong cast—where did I go <u>right</u>?"

Zero Mostel to Gene Wilder
THE PRODUCERS, 1968

327. "Out here, due process is a bullet."

John Wayne exuding charm again
THE GREEN BERETS, 1968

328. "Hello, gorgeous."

Barbra Streisand to her reflection in mirror
FUNNY GIRL, 1968

329. "How dear of you to let me out of jail."

Katharine Hepburn to Peter O'Toole
THE LION IN WINTER, 1968

330. "I told you 158 times I cannot stand little notes on my pillow. 'We are out of corn flakes. F.U.' It took me three hours to figure out F.U. was Felix Ungar. It's not your fault, Felix: it's a rotten combination, that's all."

Walter Matthau to Jack Lemmon
THE ODD COUPLE, 1968

331. "Git along little dogie for you know New York'll be your new home."

Jon Voight singing to himself
MIDNIGHT COWBOY, 1969

332. "Pardon me Ma'am — I'm new here in town and I'm lookin' for the Statue of Liberty."

"It's up in Central Park...If you hurry up, you'll catch the supper show."

Exchange between rube Jon Voight and worldly Sylvia Miles
MIDNIGHT COWBOY, 1969

333. "Yowsir! Yowsir! Yowsir! Here they are again — these wonderful, wonderful kids, still struggling, still hoping as the clock of fate ticks away. The dance of destiny continues. The marathon goes on and on and on. How long can they last? Let's hear it. C'mon, let's hear it. Let's hear it."

Gig Young emceeing dance contest
THEY SHOOT HORSES DON'T THEY, 1969

334. "Who _are_ those guys?"
    Robert Redford to Paul Newman regarding the unshakeable posse
        BUTCH CASSIDY AND THE SUNDANCE KID, 1969

335. "We've got to start thinking beyond our guns. Those days are closing fast."

> William Holden to gang
> THE WILD BUNCH, 1969

336. "Fill your hand, you son of a bitch!"

> John Wayne to Robert Duvall
> TRUE GRIT, 1969

337. "Nic, nic, nic, fire...Nic, nic, nic!"

> Jack Nicholson's drinking refrain
> EASY RIDER, 1969

338. "We blew it."

> Peter (Captain America) Fonda to Dennis Hopper
> the night before they die
> EASY RIDER, 1969

339. "Give me a girl at an impressionable age and she is mine for life."

Maggie Smith
THE PRIME OF MISS JEAN BRODIE, 1969


340. "I used to — used to make obscene phone calls to her — collect — and she used to accept the charges all the time."

Woody Allen to Janet Margolin
TAKE THE MONEY AND RUN, 1969

341. "First we'll have an orgy, then we'll go see Tony Bennett."
Elliott Gould to Natalie Wood, Robert Culp and Dyan Cannon
BOB AND CAROL AND TED AND ALICE, 1969

# THE SEVENTIES

342. "...Now all you have to do is hold the chicken, bring me the toast, give me a check for the chicken salad sandwich—and you haven't broken any rules."

> Jack Nicholson to obstinate waitress
> FIVE EASY PIECES, 1970

343. "Love means never having to say you're sorry."

> Ryan O'Neal quoting Ali MacGraw (See #360)
> LOVE STORY, 1970

344. "So what's the story?"

> Richard Castellano's frequent refrain
> LOVERS AND OTHER STRANGERS, 1970

345. "Does she smile when you mount her?"

> Dustin Hoffman
> LITTLE BIG MAN, 1970

346. "Frank, were you on this religious kick at home, or did you crack up over here?"

Donald Sutherland to Robert Duvall
M*A*S*H, 1970

347. "Anyone who wants to get out of combat isn't really crazy, so I can't ground him."

Jack Gilford to Alan Arkin
CATCH-22, 1970

348. "Rommel, you beautiful bastard, I read your book."

George C. Scott to Karl Michel Vogler
PATTON, 1970

349. "Forty-two percent of all liberals are queer. The Wallace people took a poll."

Peter Boyle
JOE, 1970

350. "Oh my <u>God</u>, George."

Sandy Dennis's frequent refrain to Jack Lemmon
THE OUT OF TOWNERS, 1970

351. "It's not as easy getting laid as it used to be."

Jack Nicholson to Art Garfunkel
CARNAL KNOWLEDGE, 1971

352. "Did you ever pick your feet in Poughkeepsie?"

Gene Hackman's pet non sequitur
THE FRENCH CONNECTION, 1971

353. "I know what you're thinking. Did he fire six shots or only five? Well, to tell you the truth, in all this excitement I've kinda lost track myself. But being this is a .44 magnum, the most powerful handgun in the world, and would blow your head clean off— you've got to ask yourself one qustion: do I feel lucky? Well, do ya, punk?"

Clint Eastwood to thug
DIRTY HARRY, 1971

354. "Men have paid $200 for me, and here you are, turning down a freebie. You could get a perfectly good dishwasher for that."

Jane Fonda to Donald Sutherland

KLUTE, 1971

355. "You've no right to call me to account. I've only come about my cough."

Peter Finch to camera<br>SUNDAY, BLOODY SUNDAY, 1971

356. "You're greedy, unfeeling, inept, indifferent, self-inflating and unconscionably profitable. Aside from that, I have nothing against you. I'm sure you play a helluva game of golf."

George C. Scott to Richard Dysart<br>THE HOSPITAL, 1971

357. "Death ends a life. But it does not end a relationship."

Gene Hackman opening and closing refrain<br>regarding his father Melvyn Douglas<br>I NEVER SANG FOR MY FATHER, 1971

358. "My father made him an offer he couldn't refuse."

Al Pacino to Diane Keaton
THE GODFATHER, 1972

359. "I hate the beach. I hate the sun. I'm pale and I'm redheaded. I don't tan — I stroke!"

Woody Allen
PLAY IT AGAIN, SAM, 1972

360. "That's the dumbest thing I ever heard..."

Ryan O'Neal to Barbra Streisand regarding
a famous line from another movie (see #343)
WHAT'S UP, DOC?, 1972

361. "<u>Willkommen</u>, <u>bienvenue</u>, welcome."

Joel Grey's opening line
CABARET, 1972

362. "Screw Max!"
    "I do!"
    "So do I."

Michael York and Liza Minnelli
regarding the bisexual Helmut Griem
CABARET, 1972


363. "I'm in spasm."

George Segal to Glenda Jackson
A TOUCH OF CLASS, 1972


364. "How 'bout coming up to my place for a spot of heavy breathing?"
Walter Matthau to Carol Burnett
PETE 'N' TILLIE, 1972


365. "Live! Otherwise you got nothing to talk about in the locker room."

Ruth Gordon to Bud Cort
HAROLD AND MAUDE, 1972

366. "I understand you want to marry my wife."

Laurence Olivier to Michael Caine
SLEUTH, 1972

367. "Wilt thou love her?"
"From the bottom of my soul to the tip of my penis — like a sun
in its brightness, the moon in its glory!"

Alastair Sim and Peter O'Toole
THE RULING CLASS, 1972

368. "When I die, in the newspapers they'll write that the sons of bitches of this world have lost their leader."

> Vincent Gardenia's pre-game pep talk
> BANG THE DRUM SLOWLY, 1973

369. "May I ask you a personal question: do you smile all the time?"

> Barbra Streisand to Robert Redford
> THE WAY WE WERE, 1973

370. "What would you like to have?"
"Sex."

> George Segal asking Susan Anspach
> what she likes on restaurant menu
> BLUME IN LOVE, 1973

371. "I—love—you."

> Suzanne Somers (the blonde in the white T-Bird)
> mouthing words (maybe!) to Richard Dreyfuss
> AMERICAN GRAFFITI, 1973

372. "Was it in the nature of a serious offense? For example, was it in the nature of a felony or a misdemeanor?"
"Well, it was in the nature of shoplifting."

Jack Nicholson and Randy Quaid
THE LAST DETAIL, 1973


373. "I'd only blow it."

Robert Redford's last line to Paul Newman
regarding his share of the take
THE STING, 1973

374. "He passed away two weeks ago and he bought the land a week ago...that's unusual."

Jack Nicholson to Faye Dunaway
CHINATOWN, 1974

375. "She's my sister and my daughter!"

> Faye Dunaway confessing to Jack Nicholson
> CHINATOWN, 1974

376. "Oh, My God! Someone's been sleeping in my dress!"

> Beatrice Arthur
> MAME, 1974

377. "Pardon me, boy, is this the Transylvania Station?"

> Gene Wilder
> YOUNG FRANKENSTEIN, 1974

378. "Is that a ten-gallon hat—or are you just enjoying the show?"

> Madeline Kahn as frontier entertainer Lily von
> Shtupp to an admirer in the audience
> BLAZING SADDLES, 1974

379. "I wasn't popular at school on account of having no personality
and not being pretty."

Sissy Spacek to Martin Sheen
BADLANDS, 1974

380. "Buried three of 'em. Good woman, bad diets."

Arthur Hunnicutt to Art Carney
HARRY AND TONTO, 1974

381. "I would be perfectly happy to have all my personal things burn
up in a fire because I don't have anything personal — nothing of
value. No, nothing personal except my <u>keys</u> you see..."

Gene Hackman on phone to his intrusive landlady
THE CONVERSATION, 1974

382. "Want me to do your hair?"

Warren Beatty's code word to Julie Christie
SHAMPOO, 1975

383. "Kiss me, pig...when I'm getting fucked, I like to get kissed a lot."
Al Pacino regarding Charles Durning's attempts to con him
DOG DAY AFTERNOON, 1975

384. "Peachy, I'm heartily ashamed for getting you killed instead of going home rich like you deserve to, on account of me being so bleedin' high and bloody mighty—can you forgive me?"
"That I can and that I do, Danny!"

Sean Connery and Michael Caine
THE MAN WHO WOULD BE KING, 1975

385. "They was giving me 10,000 watts a day, and, you know, I'm hot to trot. The next woman takes me out is going to light up like a pinball machine and pay off in silver dollars."

Jack Nicholson to other inmates
ONE FLEW OVER THE CUCKOO'S NEST, 1975

386. "I don't wanna break up the meeting, or nothing, but she's something of a cunt, isn't she?"

> Jack Nicholson regarding Louise Fletcher
> ONE FLEW OVER THE CUCKOO'S NEST, 1975

387. "We need a bigger boat."

> Roy Scheider to Robert Shaw on first sighting the shark
> JAWS, 1975

388. "Just because you have good manners doesn't mean I suddenly turn into Dale Evans."

> Ellen Burstyn to Kris Kristofferson
> ALICE DOESN'T LIVE HERE ANYMORE, 1975

389. "I mean, they gonna kill you. They gonna tear your heart out if you keep on. They gonna walk on your soul, girl....They gonna kill you in this town, girl."

> Robert DoQui to Gwen Welles
> NASHVILLE, 1975

390. "All the animals come out at night—poor skunk pussies, buggers, queens, fairies, dopers, junkies...sick, venial...some day a real rain will come and wash this scum off the street."

Robert DeNiro to his diary
TAXI DRIVER, 1976

391. "Good morning, Mr. Beale. They tell me you're a madman."
Ned Beatty to Peter Finch as Robert Duvall listens
NETWORK, 1976

392. "I want all of you to get up out of your chairs. I want you to get up right now and go to the window, open it and stick your head out and yell, 'I'm as mad as hell, and I'm not going to take this anymore!'"

Peter Finch to TV viewers
NETWORK, 1976

394. "I won't be wronged. I won't be insulted. I won't be laid a hand on. I don't do these things to others and I require the same of them."

John Wayne's last rallying cry
THE SHOOTIST, 1976

395. "It's so phony, and we have to leave New York during Christmas week, which really kills me."

Woody Allen to Diane Keaton about going to Los Angeles
ANNIE HALL, 1977

396. "Hey, don't knock masturbation. It's sex with someone I love."

Woody Allen to Diane Keaton
ANNIE HALL, 1977

397. "I mean, your life is New York City."

Diane Keaton to Woody Allen
ANNIE HALL, 1977

398. "May the Force be with you!"

Alec Guinness's frequent refrain
STAR WARS, 1977

399. "If you can make it there, you'll make it anywhere."

Liza Minnelli singing about The Big Apple
NEW YORK, NEW YORK, 1977

400. "Right over there, right over the river, it's beautiful, just beautiful.
The people are beautiful. The secretaries, you know, they shop
at Bonwit Taylor (sic). And like lunch hours are beautiful too."

Karen Lynn Gorney to John Travolta
SATURDAY NIGHT FEVER, 1977

401. "You have to think about one shot. One shot is what it's all about.
The deer has to be taken with one shot. I try to tell people that—
they don't listen."

Robert DeNiro to Christopher Walken
THE DEER HUNTER, 1978

402. "It's gonna be all right, Nickie. Shoot....<u>shoot</u>, Nickie!"

Robert DeNiro urging Christopher Walken to
pull trigger in Russian Roulette
THE DEER HUNTER, 1978

403. "Let's discuss it over lunch."

Alan Bates to Jill Clayburgh
AN UNMARRIED WOMAN, 1978

404. "I'm a zit, get it?"

John Belushi grossing out preppie types
ANIMAL HOUSE, 1978

415. "To be on the wire is life — the rest is waiting."

Roy Scheider to his Angel of Death, Jessica Lange
ALL THAT JAZZ, 1979


416. "You're just walkin' around to save funeral expenses."

Valerie Perrine to the down-and-out Robert Redford
THE ELECTRIC HORSEMAN, 1979


417. "It's been a long time between offers...Kiss me: if that's all right, then everything else will be."

Sally Field responding to Beau Bridges's marriage proposal
NORMA RAE, 1979


418. "I'm sorry that I was late, but I was busy trying to make a living, okay?"

Dustin Hoffman to Meryl Streep
KRAMER VS. KRAMER, 1979

419. "Does anybody have a valium?"

Charles Durning's frequent refrain
STARTING OVER, 1979

420. "Momma's boy, Momma's boy, I bet you're gonna cry. C'mon, Momma's boy, let's see you cry! C'mon, squirt a few. C'mon, cry. C'mon, cry! C'mon, c'mon, just a few. C'mon, squirt a few. C'mon, squirt. C'mon, cry! Cry! Cry! One-two-three, cry! C'mon, one-two-three, cry! C'mon, cry! C'mon, baby, c'mon little girl, cry...!"

Robert Duvall unmercifully baiting his son Michael O'Keefe
THE GREAT SANTINI, 1979

421. "I can feel it..."

Jack Lemmon's dying words to Jane Fonda
regarding vibrations from nuclear reactor
THE CHINA SYNDROME, 1979

422. "C'mon. You're my brother. Be friends—ya fuckin' bum. Give me a break. C'mon, kiss me. Give me a kiss. C'mon."

Robert DeNiro's belated appeal to Joe Pesci
RAGING BULL, 1980

423. "We're on a mission from God."

John Belushi and Dan Aykroyd's frequent refrain
THE BLUES BROTHERS, 1980

**424. "He-e-e-re's Johnnie!"**

Jack Nicholson to Shelley Duvall
THE SHINING, 1980

405. "Why do we always expect them to come in metal ships?"

Veronica Cartwright
INVASION OF THE BODY SNATCHERS, 1978


406. "Why are you nervous? This isn't 'Have-a-gimp-over-for-dinner-night,' is it? You're not one of <u>those</u> weirdos."

Jon Voight to Jane Fonda
COMING HOME, 1978


407. "We can walk on the moon and turn garbage into roses."
"You're a poet!"

Paul Sorvino and Anne Ditchburn
SLOW DANCING IN THE BIG CITY, 1978


408. "Left turn, Clyde."

Clint Eastwood suggesting hand signal to his chimpanzee
EVERY WHICH WAY BUT LOOSE, 1978

409. "I like to watch."

Peter Sellers' frequent refrain
BEING THERE, 1979

410. "Whenever Mrs. Kissel breaks wind, we beat the dog."

Max Showalter to Dudley Moore
regarding his housekeeper, Nedra Volz
"10," 1979


411. "Nobody made it. Nobody sold it. Nobody <u>sees</u> it. It doesn't exist."

Peter Boyle to George C. Scott regarding child porno flicks
HARDCORE, 1979


412. "No, you're not a cutter — I'm a cutter."

Dennis Christopher distinguishing himself
from the "townies"
BREAKING AWAY, 1979


413. "Fun? How would you like to go around dressed like a head waiter for the last seven hundred years?"

George Hamilton complaining about
being a vampire to Arte Johnson
LOVE AT FIRST BITE, 1979

414. "I love the smell of napalm in the morning....it smells like victory."

Robert Duvall
APOCALYPSE NOW, 1979

425. "I am not an animal!"

John Hurt
THE ELEPHANT MAN, 1980

426. "I don't want no divorce. I just want the dag'gone bedroom in the <u>back</u> of the house!"

> Sissy Spacek to Tommy Lee Jones
> COAL MINER'S DAUGHTER, 1980

427. "Joey, have you ever been in a Turkish prison?"

> Peter Graves's pederastic come-on to Rossie Harris
> AIRPLANE!, 1980

428. "Rackets, whoring, guns — it used to be beautiful!"

> Burt Lancaster recalling good ol' days
> ATLANTIC CITY, 1981

429. "I think I'll take a bath."
"I'll alert the media."

> Dudley Moore and John Gielgud
> ARTHUR, 1981

430. "Ya wanna dance or would you rather just suck face?"

Henry Fonda's octogenarian raunch to Katharine Hepburn
ON GOLDEN POND, 1981

431. "I'll tell you right now, it's going to be wonderful."

William Hurt to Sigourney Weaver
regarding their impending love-making
EYEWITNESS, 1981

432. "Snakes...why does it always have to be snakes?"

Harrison Ford
RAIDERS OF THE LOST ARK, 1981

433. "Ze soldiers are very hoppy shooting ze pipples who say that ze pipples are not hoppy."

George Hamilton
ZORRO, THE GAY BLADE, 1981

434. "You're not too bright. I like that in a man."

Kathleen Turner to William Hurt
BODY HEAT, 1981

435. "I believe God made me for a purpose. But he also made me fast. When I run, I feel His pleasure."

Ian Charleson's holy mission
CHARIOTS OF FIRE, 1981

436. "Are we having fun yet?"

Carol Burnett's oft-quoted line
FOUR SEASONS, 1981

437. "E.T. phone home."

E.T.'s tearful refrain
E.T.—THE EXTRA-TERRESTRIAL, 1982

438. "It's amazing what you can do with a cheap piece of meat if you know how to treat it."

> Paul Bartel's last line regarding
> the unidentified meal he is serving
> EATING RAOUL, 1982

439. "There's nothing more inconvenient than an old queen with a head cold."

> Robert Preston to Julie Andrews
> VICTOR/VICTORIA, 1982

440. "Live? I can't go on <u>live</u>!! I'm a movie-star — not an actor!"

> Peter O'Toole to Mark Linn-Baker
> MY FAVORITE YEAR, 1982

441. "Wake up, it's time to die."

> Brion James's sinister paradox
> BLADE RUNNER, 1982

442. "The only reason you're still living is that I never kissed you."
Charles Durning to Dustin Hoffman
TOOTSIE, 1982

443. "This is a coast, too, George. New York is a coast too."

> Soap actor Dustin Hoffman to agent Sydney Pollack
> who is on the phone to "The Coast"
> TOOTSIE, 1982

444. "I was curious. Do you have any reaction at all to my telling you that I love you?"
"...I was just inches from a clean getaway."

> Shirley MacLaine and Jack Nicholson
> TERMS OF ENDEARMENT, 1983

445. "Goddamn it, I'd piss on a spark plug if I thought it would do any good!"

> Erik Stern to Matthew Broderick
> regarding avoiding nuclear holocaust
> WARGAMES, 1983

446. "You have been guests in our home long enough. Now we would like you to leave."

> Ben Kingsley to British authorities
> GANDHI, 1983

447. "We all have our little sorrows, Ducky. You're not the only one. The littler you are, the larger the sorrow. You think you loved him?...What about <u>me</u>!"

Tom Courtenay to Zena Walker over Albert Finney's corpse
THE DRESSER, 1983

448. "Go ahead, make my day."

Clint Eastwood to punk
SUDDEN IMPACT, 1983

449. "We came, we saw, we kicked its ass!"

Harold Ramis, Dan Aykroyd and Bill Murray
to concerned New Yorkers
GHOSTBUSTERS, 1984

450. "You hear me New York? We're gonna be on Broadway, because we're not giving up. I'm still here and I'm staying. You hear that New York? The frog is staying!"

A determined Kermit the Frog
THE MUPPETS TAKE MANHATTAN, 1984

451. "I can't believe I gave my panties to a geek."

Molly Ringwald about Anthony Michael Hall
SIXTEEN CANDLES, 1984

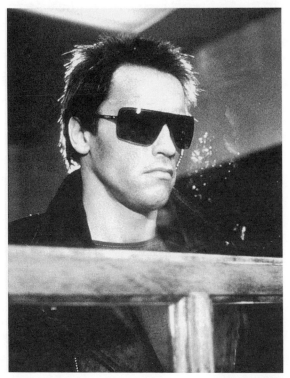

452. "I'll be back..."

Arnold Schwarzenegger
THE TERMINATOR, 1984

453. "Welcome to the Statue of Liberty. The statue was a gift from French citizens. It has come to symbolize hope for naked women everywhere."

> Discombobulated tourist guide Fred Ganz to tourists upon seeing Daryl Hannah emerge naked from the Hudson River
> SPLASH, 1984

454. "This is New York City. A man can do whatever he wants."

> NYPD cop to KGB agent trying to prevent Robin Williams's defection in Bloomingdale's
> MOSCOW ON THE HUDSON, 1984

455. "Ya can't <u>learn</u> to be real. It's like learning to be a midget. It's not something you can learn."

> Jeff Daniels to his double
> THE PURPLE ROSE OF CAIRO, 1985

456. "Come on, Chawley. Ya wanna do it? Let's do it, right here on the Oriental."

> Anjelica Huston to Jack Nicholson
> PRIZZI'S HONOR, 1985

457. "I wanna be just like you...all I need is a lobotomy and some tights."
Judd Nelson (right) to varsity wrestler Emilio Estevez
THE BREAKFAST CLUB, 1985

458. "I used to sit on our front gallery every morning and every evening just to nod hello to Roy John Murray."

Geraldine Page's poignant nostalgia to Rebecca DeMornay
THE TRIP TO BOUNTIFUL, 1985


459. "I've seen the future! It's a bald headed man from New York!"

Albert Brooks suffering from Yuppie hysteria
LOST IN AMERICA, 1985


460. "You know, if you shoot me you'll lose a lot of these humanitarian awards."

Chevy Chase to police chief
FLETCH, 1985

**461. "If this is foreplay, I'm a dead man!"**
Steve Guttenberg to the seductive alien Tahnee Welch
COCOON, 1985

**462. "I know you are, but what am I?"**
Pee-wee Herman's withering comeback to Mark Holton's taunts
PEE-WEE'S BIG ADVENTURE, 1985

463. "It's just a romance, but it's <u>so</u> beautiful."
William Hurt to Raul Julia regarding his version of his movie
**KISS OF THE SPIDER WOMAN, 1985**

464. "You should have asked permission."
"I did. She said yes."

> Klaus-Maria Brandauer and Robert Redford
> in classic exchange regarding Meryl Streep
> OUT OF AFRICA, 1985

465. "How in the hell would I know why there are Nazis? I don't know how this can opener works."

> Leo Postrel to Woody Allen
> HANNAH AND HER SISTERS, 1986

466. "Cameron's so tight if you stuck a piece of coal up his ass in two weeks you'd have a diamond."

> Matthew Broderick to camera
> FERRIS BUELLER'S DAY OFF, 1986

467. "There are plenty of fine, superfine women in New York."

John Canada Terrell
SHE'S GOT TO HAVE IT, 1986

468. "Why did you put your head in the oven?"
"Oh, I don't know, Meg....I'm havin' a bad day—it's been a real bad day."

Jessica Lange and Sissy Spacek
CRIMES OF THE HEART, 1986

469. "Imagine! Seven million people all wantin' to live together! Yup—New York must be the friendliest place on earth."

Paul Hogan to incredulous limo driver Reginald VelJohnson
CROCODILE DUNDEE, 1986

470. "How you getting along with the New Yorkers?"
"Fun's a people, friendly, full of beans—but weird!"

Australia-to-New York phone conversation
between Jon Meillon and Paul Hogan
CROCODILE DUNDEE, 1986

471. "I'm being marked down? I've been kidnapped by K-Mart!"

Bette Midler to Helen Slater regarding her reduced ransom
RUTHLESS PEOPLE, 1986


472. "Get away from her, you bitch!"

Sigourney Weaver to alien queen regarding the orphan
ALIENS, 1986


473. "Bring a pitcher of beer every seven minutes until someone passes out, then bring one every ten minutes."

Rodney Dangerfield to waitress
BACK TO SCHOOL, 1986

474. "They're ba-ack!"

Heather O'Rourke into telephone receiver
POLTERGEIST II: THE OTHER SIDE, 1986

475. "If you could do it all again, Gramps, what would you do different?"
"I'd have taken better care of my teeth."

Kathleen Turner and Leon Ames
PEGGY SUE GOT MARRIED, 1986

476. "I make it a policy never to have sex before the first date."

Sally Field laying down the law to Michael Caine
SURRENDER, 1987

477. "My name is Inigo Montoya. You killed my father — prepare to die!"

Mandy Patinkin to Chris Sarandon
PRINCESS BRIDE, 1987

478. "No matter where you go or what you do, you're gonna die."

Olympia Dukakis straightening out Vincent Gardenia
about his philandering
MOONSTRUCK, 1987

479. "I'll be takin' these Huggies and...uh, whatever cash you got."

Nicolas Cage holding up convenience store
in dual role of father and hood
RAISING ARIZONA, 1987

480. "Greed is good! Greed is right! Greed works! Greed will save the U.S.A.!"

Michael Douglas sounding Yuppie credo to stockholders
WALL STREET, 1987

481. "Whaddya got on the West Side — Sean and Madonna?"

Sylvia Miles to Charlie Sheen
WALL STREET, 1987

482. "I see your schwartz is as big as mine. Now let's see how well you handle it."

> Rick Moranis to Bill Pullman regarding their light-sabers
> SPACEBALLS, 1987

483. "Do it!"

> Tom Berenger telling Charlie Sheen to shoot him
> PLATOON, 1987

484. "Except for socially, you're my role model."

> Joan Cusack to Holly Hunter
> BROADCAST NEWS, 1987

485. "If anything happens to me tell every woman I've ever gone out with I was talking about her at the end. That way they'll have to re-evaluate me."

Albert Brooks to Holly Hunter
BROADCAST NEWS, 1987

486. "I won't be ignored."

Glenn Close making it painfully clear to Michael Douglas
FATAL ATTRACTION, 1987

487. "Don't kill me. I'm basically a good kid."

Corey Haim to Jason Patric
THE LOST BOYS, 1987

488. "Goo-od morning, Vietnam!"

Robin Williams's D J signature line
GOOD MORNING, VIETNAM, 1987

489. "We can go to Roseland. I hear that's <u>tres</u> hip."

Peter Riegert to Amy Irving
CROSSING DELANCY, 1988


490. "I've seen 'The Exorcist' about 167 times!"

Otherwordly Michael Keaton to newly dead
Geena Davis and Alec Baldwin
BEETLEJUICE, 1988

491. "This is the damndest season I ever seen: the Durham Bulls can't lose and I can't get laid."

Susan Sarandon to herself
BULL DURHAM, 1988

492. "It's the only game where a black man can wave a stick at a white
    man without starting a riot."
                    Gene Hackman to Willem Dafoe regarding baseball
                    MISSISSIPPI BURNING, 1988

493. "I'm not bad, I'm just drawn that way."
        Jessica Rabbit (Kathleen Turner's voice) to Bob Hoskins
        WHO FRAMED ROGER RABBIT, 1988

494. "But where in New York can you find a woman with grace, taste, elegance and culture — a woman fit for a king?"
"Queens."

Eddie Murphy and Arsenio Hall
COMING TO AMERICA, 1988

495. "Let 'em have those princely robes. We're in New York — now let's dress like New Yorkers."

Eddie Murphy to Arsenio Hall donning Yankees warm-up
jackets after their royal luggage has been ripped-off
COMING TO AMERICA, 1988

496. "Sometimes I sing and dance around my house in my underwear. That doesn't make me Madonna."

Joan Cusack to Melanie Griffith
WORKING GIRL, 1988

497. "Don't call me stupid!"

Kevin Kline's frequent refrain
A FISH CALLED WANDA, 1988

498. "I love New York. It's like a thousand comedy lines looking for a straight line."

> Alan Alda
> CRIMES AND MISDEMEANORS, 1989

499. "How do you like New York so far?"
"Hey, it's my kinda town."

> John Travolta and "Baby Mikey" (Bruce Willis's voice)
> LOOK WHO'S TALKING, 1989

500. "What are you laughing at?"

> Jack Nicholson to gargoyle
> BATMAN, 1989

# THE NINETIES

501. "Ditto…"

> Patrick Swayze's reticent affirmation
> of love to Demi Moore
> GHOST, 1990

## About the Author

When he is not watching movies, John P. Fennell is a free-lance writer and editor. He has worked as a movie consultant and researcher for advertising agencies and film libraries. For twenty years John taught English, history, and drama in New York City and elsewhere. He founded the Celestial Playhouse, a drama workshop for young people, and has written and directed a score of original plays for stage, including *The Lonely Clone, Gewgaw's Bauble,* and *Uncle Wally's Problem,* which have enjoyed successful productions in Santa Fe, New Mexico. John is also the author of a half-dozen as yet unproduced screenplays including *Ghost Writer, Hail to the Chief,* and *The Late Great Harry Ball* (a movie about movies), which are currently making the rounds in Hollywood. John and his wife Nancy live in Tucson, Arizona.